DIGITAL FORENSICS

DIGITAL FORENSICS

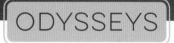

VALERIE BODDEN

CREATIVE EDUCATION · CREATIVE PAPERBACKS

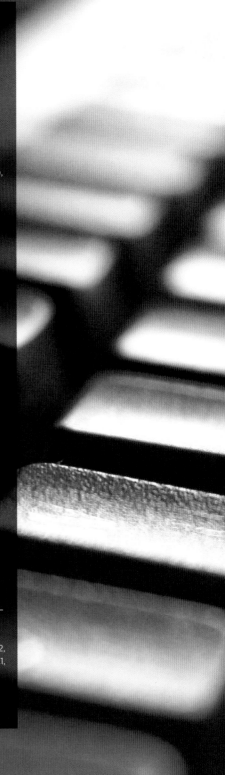

Published by Creative Education and Creative Paperbacks
P.O. Box 227, Mankato, Minnesota 56002
Creative Education and Creative Paperbacks
are imprints of The Creative Company
www.thecreativecompany.us

Design by Blue Design (www.bluedes.com)
Production by Joe Kahnke
Art direction by Rita Marshall
Printed in China

Photographs by Alamy (Anthony Brown, epa european
pressphoto agency b.v., Graham Hughes, Tommy E Trenchard),
Dreamstime (Viappy), Federal Bureau of Investigation (FBI.
gov/U.S. Department of Justice/U.S. Government), Flickr
(makototakeuchi), Getty Images (Bloomberg, CBS Photo
Archive, MICHAEL THURSTON), Immigration and Customs
Enforcement (ICE/Department of Homeland Security/U.S.
Government), iStockphoto (DragonImages, jeka1984,
maciek905, Baran Özdemir), Newscom (Angelika Warmuth/
dpa/picture-alliance, zuma), Shutterstock (bioraven, Chera,
Korn, mirtmirt, quka, TFoxFoto, Jiri Vaclavek, John Williams
RUS)

Library of Congress Cataloging-in-Publication Data
Names: Bodden, Valerie, author.
Title: Digital forensics / Valerie Bodden.
Series: Odysseys in crime scene science.
Includes bibliographical references and index.
Summary: An in-depth look at how digital forensic examiners
analyze devices with forensic tools to prevent cybercrimes
and catch criminals, employing real-life examples such as the
BTK killer case.

Identifiers: LCCN 2015027600 / ISBN 978-1-60818-680-8
(hardcover) / ISBN 978-1-62832-469-3 (pbk) / ISBN 978-1-
56660-716-2 (eBook)

Subjects: LCSH: 1. Computer crimes—Juvenile literature.
2. Computer crimes—Investigation—Juvenile literature.
3. Forensic sciences—Juvenile literature.
Classification: LCC HV8079.C65 B63 2016 / DDC 363.25/968—
dc23

CCSS: RI 8.1, 2, 3, 4, 5, 8, 10; RI 9-10.1, 2, 3, 4, 5, 8, 10; RI 11-12.1, 2,
3, 4, 5, 10; RST 6-8.1, 2, 5, 6, 10; RST 9-10.1, 2, 5, 6, 10; RST 11-12.1,
2, 5, 6, 10

First Edition HC 9 8 7 6 5 4 3 2 1
First Edition PBK 9 8 7 6 5 4 3 2 1

CONTENTS

Introduction 9

All Kinds of Crimes 11

Even Criminals Use Social Media 21

Cracking the Computer 24

Hidden in Plain Sight 33

It's All Connected 37

The Many Hats of Hackers 41

Cyber Fiction 50

Sony, North Korea, and *The Interview* 56

Keeping Up with the Digital World 65

You Be the Analyst 67

Glossary 77

Selected Bibliography 78

Websites 79

Index .80

Introduction

Blue and red lights sweep across the front of a home. They reflect off jagged shards of glass in a broken first-floor window. Inside, books and pictures have been tossed to the floor. Papers hang from ransacked drawers. Two plates—their food still warm—sit on the kitchen table. A small red spot stains the floor under one of the chairs. This looks like a crime scene. But by the time police

OPPOSITE: When police officers arrive at a crime scene, they create a barrier to prevent unauthorized access to—and contamination of—the scene. Using crime scene tape, barricades, and police cars, they cordon off the area until investigators have finished processing it.

arrived, the house was empty. Now investigators must use crime scene science to help solve the mystery of what happened here—and who did it.

Crime scene science is also referred to as forensic science. Forensic science is simply science that is used to solve crimes and provide facts in a legal trial. Solving a crime often involves many forensic scientists, each specializing in a different area. Today, in almost any crime, some of those forensic scientists are likely to be digital forensics examiners. These experts analyze computers, cell phones, and other digital devices. They look for evidence of crimes from fraud to murder. What they find might just be the key to solving the case.

All Kinds of Crimes

For criminals, computers have made some crimes easier to commit than ever before. Rather than holding up a bank, robbers can now steal millions of dollars from the comfort of their home. "The modern thief can steal more with a computer than with a gun," concluded a report by the National Academy of Sciences (NAS). Fortunately, computers have also

With digital devices everywhere, digital evidence is the new DNA.

given law enforcement new tools with which to collect evidence.

The process of digital forensics involves finding, processing, and analyzing evidence from any digital device. Computers, cell phones, tablets, digital cameras, MP3 players, GPS units, printers, and even gaming consoles are fair game. With digital devices everywhere, digital evidence "is the new DNA," according to forensic analyst Ira Victor.

Every time a person uses a digital device, he is "leaving a trail, albeit a digital one," says John Sammons, a professor of digital forensics. "Like a coating of fresh snow, these [devices] capture our 'footprints' as we go about

our daily life. Cell phone records, ATM transactions, Web searches, e-mails, and text messages are a few of the footprints we leave." These digital footprints can be used in a number of ways. They can prove that a crime has happened. Or they can confirm witness testimony or an alibi. They often serve as circumstantial evidence. And in some cases, they even establish guilt.

According to investigators, almost any crime can be associated with some sort of digital evidence. Some murderers take pictures of their victims, for example. Or someone might videotape an assault. Burglars might use an online mapping program or a GPS unit to locate their victim's house. Drug dealers might keep a computer spreadsheet of their sales. Or they might arrange a drug deal through e-mail or an Internet chat room.

In addition to providing evidence related to traditional crimes, digital devices are also key elements of cybercrimes. These crimes are committed online or through a computer network. Downloading copyrighted movies or music is a crime called copyright infringement. Tricking people into buying things is also easy to do online. From 2004 to 2009, for example, Icarus Dakota Ferris sold fake postage stamps online. He made more than $345,000 before his arrest. Cyberbullying—using websites, social media, e-mails, or other digital media to make fun of or insult someone—is a growing problem. In the United States, about half of all states now include cyberbullying in their anti-bullying laws. But only 18 states have criminal punishments for bullying.

Many cybercriminals target computers to attack a network or access people's passwords or financial data. Hackers, for example, look for ways to break into a computer system. Once inside, they might commit cybervandalism. That's what members of the group Hacking for Girlies did. In 1998, they took over the *New York Times* website. They replaced news articles with their own content and demanded the release of jailed hacker Kevin Mitnick.

Other hackers break into the computer networks of credit card companies, hospitals, and even schools to steal personal information. They might then sell that information or use it to make credit card

purchases or to steal identities. In 2013, for example, hackers broke into the computer system of retail giant Target. They stole the credit card information of 40 million Target customers.

Some criminals use phishing to gain information without hacking. Usually, this involves sending an e-mail that looks like it is from a legitimate bank. The message tells the individual to follow a certain link to update his account information. Clicking on the link takes him to a bogus site. The site collects the user's password and other information. The criminal can then use this information to access the user's account on the real site.

Criminals can also gain access to personal information through malware (short for "malicious software"). Spyware is a kind of malware that can track a person's computer activity. Some spyware includes keyloggers that keep track of a user's keystrokes. The software can capture usernames, passwords, and even account numbers. Viruses and worms are also kinds of malware. Sometimes malware is used to damage computers and computer networks. In 1999, for example, the Melissa virus spread through 20 percent of computers in the world. It caused millions of dollars in damage to computer systems. The virus overwrote document files in infected computers with quotes from the TV show *The Simpsons*. E-mail servers around the world had to shut down to stop the virus's spread.

The first step in any computer forensics investigation is collecting evidence. This may be carried out by police officers, crime scene investigators (CSIs), or digital forensics examiners. Whoever collects the evidence looks for any device that could hold information. This could

Once a piece of evidence is located, the investigator has to be careful not to change it in any way.

include gaming consoles and tiny memory cards. There might also be thumb drives disguised as pens, knives, or even sushi.

Once a piece of evidence is located, the investigator has to be careful not to change it in any way. This means if a computer is turned off, it should be left off. If it is on, the keyboard should not be pressed, and the mouse should not be clicked. Doing so could alter the device's data logs. The investigator should take pictures of the computer's screen. Then, if possible, a digital forensics examiner might complete an analysis on-site.

More often, though, the computer is unplugged and

Even Criminals Use Social Media

Today, when police want to know more about a suspect, they don't just check mug shots and criminal histories. They also turn to social media sites such as Facebook or Twitter. These sites can provide information about a suspect's education, friends, and favorite places. Sometimes, they also provide direct evidence of a crime as people post about their exploits. In other cases, social media is used to commit crimes. A group of teenage girls in California tracked the locations of celebrities on Twitter in 2009. Then they burglarized the celebrities' homes while they were out. Victims included Paris Hilton and Lindsay Lohan. Social media has also been used to organize flash mobs. Participants communicate beforehand and seem to appear out of nowhere for an unanticipated performance. But even these fun events can turn violent.

taken back to the lab for evaluation. Because digital devices are so sensitive, they need to be packed in antistatic bags. These bags are made of special materials that prevent static shocks from damaging the device. Electronic devices also have to be kept away from magnets, moisture, and extreme temperatures. Cell phones are placed in special antistatic bags known as Faraday bags. These keep signals from being sent or received by the phone.

As an investigator works, she records what was collected, where, when, and by whom. This helps to establish the chain of custody. The chain of custody is a log of who has the evidence at all times and what they do with it. At the lab, the evidence needs to be locked up so that it cannot be accessed—and possibly tampered with—by unauthorized individuals.

Cracking the Computer

The digital devices seized from a crime scene contain original evidence. Anything an investigator does with these devices could alter them. Even something as simple as turning them on or opening a file can cause changes. That is why digital forensics experts do not work directly on original evidence except in emergency situations, such as a missing-child case.

Instead, they make a copy of the evidence and analyze the copy.

Simply copying and pasting data from an original drive onto a new one cannot get investigators all the information they need. This would provide only active data—those files and folders that users can access. But investigators also want information that isn't visible to users. This includes system logs and deleted files. To get this information, investigators need to use special forensic software programs called forensic tools. A forensic tool can make an exact copy of every **bit** the drive contains. The copy is known as a forensic image.

To create a forensic image, the original drive is connected to a blank hard drive. Before information can be copied, a write blocker must be installed between the two drives. This is a piece of hardware or software that prevents anything from being written to the original drive. It ensures that the original evidence is not altered during the imaging process. Depending on the size of the original drive, imaging can take several hours to complete.

Once the forensic image is made, the examiner has to check that it is an exact copy. To do this, he uses a process called hashing. Hashing uses mathematical **algorithms** to convert data into a unique set of letters and numbers called a hash value. The forensic tool creates a hash value for both the original evidence

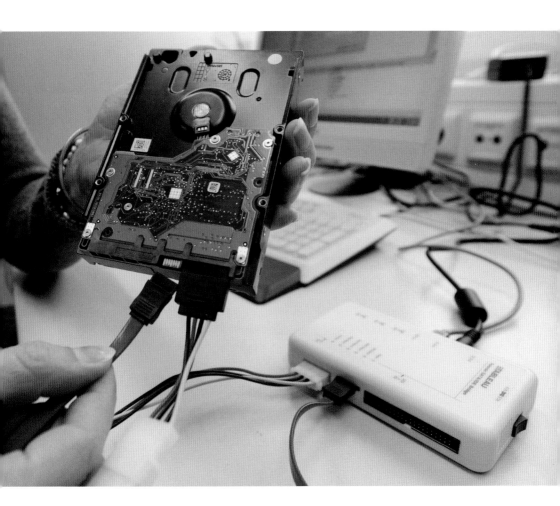

and the forensic image. If the hash values are the same, it indicates that the two drives are identical. If even one bit is different between the two drives, the hash values will not match. Hashing is so specific to a particular data set that it is often referred to as digital DNA or digital fingerprinting.

Once a forensic image has been created, the digital forensics examiner can begin to analyze it. One of the most obvious places to look for evidence is computer files created by the user. These can include documents, spreadsheets, e-mails, photos, and calendars. Not all user-created files are easy to find. Suspects often delete incriminating documents or images. But when someone deletes a computer file, that file is not removed from the computer's memory. The file remains where it is, but a link to it can no longer be found in the file directory. The

When someone deletes a computer file, that file is not removed from the computer's memory.

computer considers the space where the file is stored unallocated, or free, space. This means that it can be overwritten—a new file can be saved over it. However, until it is overwritten, the original file can be accessed by forensic tools.

Even once a deleted file is overwritten, some data may still be available. Computers store data in fixed-size blocks of memory. If the new file is smaller than the original, it will not fill the entire memory block. Any part of the block not needed by the new file will still contain the original data. The space containing that original data is known as slack space. Forensic software can be used to access it.

nstead of deleting files, criminals may simply try to block access to them. They may encrypt a document, for example. To encrypt a file, a code is used to scramble the text so that it cannot be read. The file can only be decrypted, or unscrambled, with a decryption key or password. A digital forensics examiner might use a software program to try to crack the file's password. Using such a program can be risky, however. The suspect may have set up a fail-safe to destroy data if too many incorrect passwords are entered.

Information contained in files is not the only useful evidence a computer forensics examiner can find. Whenever you create a file, the computer assigns metadata to that file. Metadata is data about data. It includes information about the computer owner, the author of the file, and the date and time the file was created or modified.

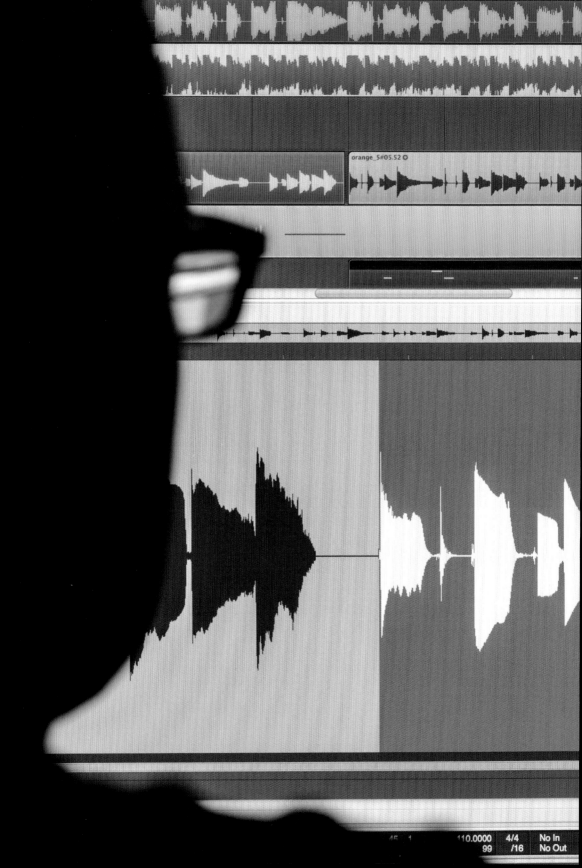

orange_5#05.52

45   1   110.0000   4/4   No In
99   /16   No Out

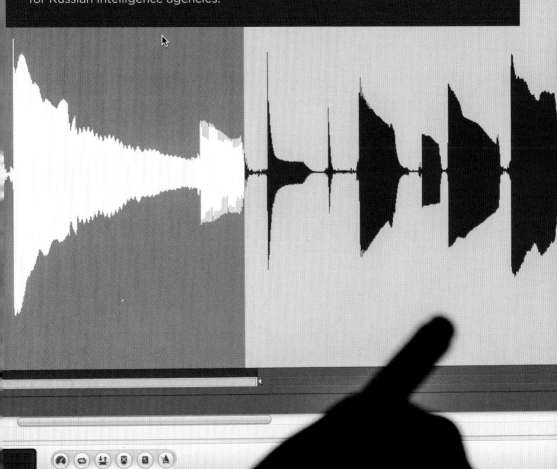

Hidden in Plain Sight

Sometimes, encrypted data is hidden in images, sounds, or other computer files. This is done through a process known as steganography. The encrypted data is inserted into the least important bits of a file. In the case of an image, this might affect the color quality. But the change is not enough to be noticeable. The image is then posted on a website or sent via e-mail. Special software is needed to extract the hidden message. Today, there are nearly 1,000 steganography programs available online. Many are free. Steganography is generally difficult to detect, but in June 2010, the Federal Bureau of Investigation (FBI) arrested 11 suspected Russian spies. The spies had been using steganography to hide data for Russian intelligence agencies.

This information can establish a link between a suspect and a crime. This happened in the case of the BTK killer. Between 1974 and 1991, BTK killed 10 people in and around Wichita, Kansas, but was never caught. Over the years, he would send the police taunting letters. Then, in 2005, he sent a computer disk to a Wichita television station. Police examined the disk's metadata and found a deleted file that had been created on a computer at a local church. The author of the document was listed as "Dennis." Police quickly learned that a man named Dennis Rader was the president of the church's council. DNA evidence confirmed that Rader was the BTK killer.

The computer registry can also be a rich source of evidence. The registry includes information about what is happening on the computer. Event logs, for example, track programs used, computer errors, and login attempts.

The computer also tracks Internet use. When you visit a website, your computer saves a temporary Internet file of the site. That way, the next time you visit, the site will load faster. In addition, the most recent addresses you've typed directly into the search bar are saved. A log file also tracks how many times you've visited each site. Your browsing history and search terms are stored as well. Investigators can use these items as circumstantial evidence in a case. For example, in 2007, Melanie McGuire was convicted of sedating and killing her husband and dumping his body in the Chesapeake Bay. Among the evidence presented were Internet searches McGuire had recently performed. She had looked up "undetected poisons," "how to commit murder," and "how to buy a gun in Pennsylvania."

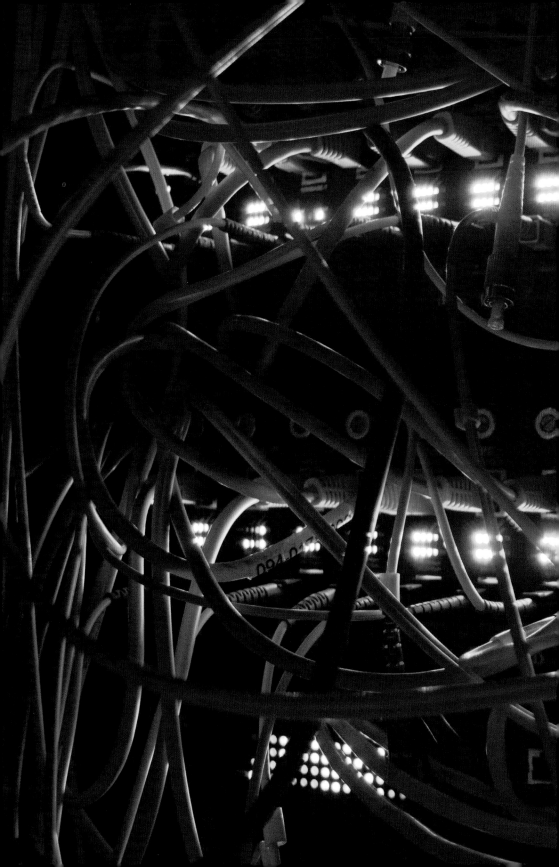

It's All Connected

In most cases, digital forensics examiners analyze data after a crime has occurred. But in some cases, they may need to analyze an active computer. Such analysis is known as incident response, or live analysis. It is often used to detect and analyze network attacks and malware.

Live analysis gives examiners access to volatile artifacts. These are bits of digital information that exist only while a computer is running. Network

OPPOSITE: A network is a group of computers connected with hardware or software. Networked devices can share large amounts of data with ease. The first computer network, the Advanced Research Projects Agency Network (ARPANET), was created for the U.S. Department of Defense.

connections, running processes, and entered passwords are all types of volatile artifacts. Most volatile artifacts exist in the computer's **random-access memory (RAM)**. RAM requires a constant power source to maintain its memory. As soon as the power source is removed, the data in RAM begins to fade.

any big companies and governmental departments have been the victims of network attacks. In 2011, for example, an international crime group broke into the network of Fidelity National Information

Services, a prepaid credit card company, and stole $13 million in one day. Not all network attacks come from outside a company, though. Sometimes, employees use their network access to **embezzle** money, steal trade secrets, or otherwise harm a company. In one case, a systems administrator designed a program that destroyed software worth $10 million after he was fired.

Investigating network issues can be a difficult and lengthy process. Evidence can be spread across multiple devices. It might be on employee computers, servers, **routers**, printers, and other devices. Investigators attempt to track the movements of the attacker through the network using event logs from these devices.

The largest network in the world, by far, is the Internet. It connects billions of computers and other devices. Fraud, child pornography, hacking, malware,

The Many Hats of Hackers

Hacking started in the 1960s as a way to improve computer performance. By the 1980s, hackers were carrying out the first malicious attacks against computer networks. Today, computer hackers are identified as "black-hat," "white-hat," or "gray-hat." The goal of white-hat hackers is to seek out flaws in security systems. They are often hired by companies to test network security by trying to break in. Black-hat hackers, on the other hand, are those who hack in harmful ways. Their hacking is usually illegal. Gray-hat hackers fall somewhere in between. Like black-hat hackers, their hacks are usually performed without permission, sometimes illegally. But like white-hat hackers, their purpose is to identify security issues. They then report those issues to systems administrators

E-mails can serve as great sources of evidence because people often say things in them that they would never say in real life.

cyberbullying, and other crimes are all common on the Internet. Fortunately, the Internet provides ways for digital forensics examiners to track criminals as well. Examiners can trace the Internet Protocol (IP) address of the computer used to commit a crime. An IP address is a unique number assigned to a specific network, computer, or device on the Internet. Sometimes tracking an IP address proves to be fruitless, since hackers can spoof, or fake, their IP address.

Like the Internet, e-mail can be a double-edged sword. Criminals may use e-mails to **extort** money from individuals or businesses. In 2000, Oleg Zezev hacked into the network of the financial information firm Bloomberg. He then e-mailed threats to disclose the security breach unless the firm paid him $200,000. E-mails are also used to commit fraud or identity theft. Some criminals use e-mails to arrange drug deals or send illicit photographs.

E-mails can serve as great sources of evidence because people often say things in them that they would never say in real life. In addition, e-mails are relatively easy to find in places other than personal computers. E-mails can also be found on company backup files, smartphones, or any server that the message passed through after it was sent. The header of an e-mail can also help investigators track a criminal. The header contains the IP addresses of both the sender and receiver of a message. It also lists all the servers the message passed through on the way to its destination. Investigators can use this information to physically locate the general area the message was sent from. Criminals can get around this, however. They might use a foreign e-mail account or anonymous remailers. These services forward an e-mail without revealing the sender's IP address.

Of course, computers are not the only devices used to browse the Internet or send e-mails. Today, people are using smartphones and tablets for these tasks and more. Attorney Don Kohtz and digital forensics expert Matt Churchill have called cell phones "the new evidentiary gold mine." Recovering data from a phone can be even more difficult than getting it from a computer, though. This is largely because there are greater varieties of cell phones and operating systems. "There is such a wide variety when dealing with mobile devices that it is impossible to be well-versed in every single operating structure," said digital forensics specialist Christopher Vance. "There is no 'super tool' that works on every device." Whenever possible, the digital forensics examiner makes a forensic image of the device. If software to copy a particular phone does not exist, the examiner has to perform a live analysis. He must take careful notes and photographs of each step.

Phones can provide investigators with call logs, text messages, and contact lists. These can all be used to show

Thumb drives, commonly called USB or flash drives, come in a variety of storage capacities. The drives can be used to backup digital devices or to transfer files from one device to another.

a connection between a suspect and the victim or between one suspect and another. In addition, suspects may use their phone's camera to record a crime. In one case in New Jersey, for example, three teens beat a young man to death. A fourth used his phone to record the murder. Photographs taken with a phone often have metadata that includes GPS coordinates. Such coordinates can help police find a kidnapping victim. They can even lead police to where a murder victim is buried.

GPS devices on phones can also be used to track the location of the phone. Even phones whose GPS has been disabled can be tracked. Whenever a phone comes in range of a cellular antenna, that antenna makes a connection with the phone. Data from the three nearest cell phone towers can be combined to figure out an approximate location.

Digital forensics sometimes involves enhancing visual or audio evidence. With surveillance cameras placed in businesses, parking lots, and even traffic intersections, many crimes are caught on video. In addition, many crimes are captured by bystanders using smartphones. When it is clear enough, video evidence can reveal license plate numbers or even suspects' faces. Unfortunately for investigators, video quality is often poor. Using special software, examiners can lighten or darken the image, sharpen it, reduce graininess, and even stabilize any movement in the video. The audio quality of the video can also be improved by removing (or enhancing, depending on the need) background noise.

Cyber Fiction

The modern computer is a
relatively new innovation. That
means digital forensics has only
recently begun to figure in crime
fiction. Even so, it makes its share
of appearances. The 1983 movie
War Games was among the first to
highlight hacking. In it, a teenage
boy accidentally hacks into a U.S.
military computer and almost
starts a world war. In 1995, the
movie *Hackers* brought new

attention to computer security. It featured a former hacker who has to track down evidence of a dangerous new virus. In the 2007 movie *Live Free or Die Hard*, a group of cyberterrorists attempts to shut down the entire U.S. computer network.

TV crime dramas such as *NCIS* and *CSI* generally revolve around traditional forensic evidence such as fingerprints. But digital evidence plays a role as well. On one episode of the show *Criminal Minds*, for example, an FBI team searches for a missing four-year-old girl.

They notice that a suspect used the phrase "light bug" in a statement. An online search for the term brings them to an adoption forum in which a user wrote the same phrase. The evidence leads the team straight to the missing girl.

n 2015, *CSI: Cyber* was launched. As the name implies, the show centered on cybercrime. Its main character, FBI cyberpsychologist Avery Ryan, was inspired by the show's producer, a real-life cyberpsychologist named Mary Aiken. According to Aiken, "Cyberpsychology is the study of the impact of emerging technology on human behavior." On the show, Ryan's team included other digital forensics experts. A former hacker is also recruited to "hack for good" instead of being sent to prison. In the season premiere, the team investigated a series of infant abductions. The criminals cased their targets by hacking baby monitors connected to the Internet. The first season also included the investigation of a roller coaster crash caused by tampering with the ride's computer. Another episode featured cyberbullying. Some of these crimes were taken straight from present-day headlines. Real-life hackers have broken into Web-connected baby monitors, for example (although not necessarily to kidnap children). According to digital security expert Kevin Epstein, *CSI: Cyber* did "a reasonably good job of portraying to the public that Internet-connected devices are susceptible to hacking."

Even with the most advanced software, decrypting a file can take up to a year.

Although TV crime shows might get the *types* of cybercrimes right, most digital forensics experts say that many other aspects are inaccurate. The biggest difference between TV and real-life digital forensics is probably the amount of time involved. "Cyber forensic analysis doesn't move at the speed of a TV show," said Ivan Shefrin, a computer security expert. "While it can take minutes or less for a hacker to penetrate a home computer, the process of gathering and analyzing computer and network forensic evidence unfortunately takes much longer." Even with the most advanced software, decrypting a file can take up to a year. But on one episode of *CSI: Cyber*, an analyst was able to crack a 20-character password with

CYBER CRIME
DIVISION

DIGITAL FORENSICS

Sony, North Korea, and *The Interview*

In November 2014, Sony Pictures suffered a massive cyberattack. Its computer network was disabled and several unreleased movies and private e-mails were leaked. The attack was traced back to IP addresses in North Korea. At the time, Sony was weeks away from releasing the comedy film *The Interview*. The movie was about two television hosts recruited by the CIA to assassinate North Korean leader Kim Jong Un. In addition to the cyberattack, the hackers made threats against movie theaters scheduled to show the film. In response, Sony at first canceled the release. That decision was later reversed at the urging of U.S. president Barack Obama. The film came out in 330 theaters on Christmas Day 2014, grossing $1 million on its first day.

a single guess.

Real-life digital forensics experts can spend days or weeks trying to find and understand malware on a device. But on *CSI: Cyber*, the task took only about 30 seconds. That's because the good code was written in green text. The malware was red. This, of course, is not the case in real life. "Who needs source code review tools if this exists?" questioned Kaue Pena, a software security consultant.

The use of image enhancement on TV often goes beyond real-life image enhancement as well. On one episode of *CSI: New York*, for example, detectives enhance a photograph to reveal a smeared stamp on a victim's hand. The Forensic Outreach team, an educational group based in London, criticized the "seemingly endless ability of TV forensics to take the blurriest piece of [video surveillance] and expand it to reveal license plates, written data, or the reflection of a killer in a shop window.... This just can't happen in real life." That's because a photograph or video is made up of a set number of **pixels**. Magnifying the image increases the size but not the number of pixels. So it cannot make the image clearer or reveal "hidden" information.

In addition, most forensic crime shows involve far more physical action than real-life forensic scientists ever see. Journalist Lily Hay Newman explained why. "Since watching people try to trace malware or crack encryption keys is visually boring..., [*CSI: Cyber*] adds chase scenes, sniper attacks, underwater rescues, and suspect interrogations to keep things moving."

Some in the legal community worry that such deviations from reality might lead to unrealistic expectations in real life. The public, for example, may be led to believe that they understand digital forensics based on what they've seen on television. After the Boston Marathon bombing in April 2013, many people online attempted to analyze photographs of the event. These self-appointed investigators named one person after another as suspects. Journalist Laura Miller was fascinated by the "apparently widespread assumption that the average person screwing around on the Internet is well-equipped to conduct forensics analysis of photographs" just because they've watched *CSI*. Others have worried that shows like *CSI* lead jurors to expect forensic evidence in every case, even when it might not be relevant.

Digital forensics examiners testified during the trial of Dzhokhar Tsarnaev, who was convicted in the 2013 Boston Marathon bombing. The experts spoke about such evidence as search histories and downloaded files on the Tsarnaev brothers' computers, cell phones, and external hard drives.

Despite such criticisms, some in the digital forensics community have praised shows like *CSI: Cyber* for drawing attention to computer security. "Companies are getting hacked over and over," said Branden Spikes, a computer security expert, "so I think mainstream TV highlighting security as an important thing is a pleasure." Anthony Zuiker, creator of the *CSI* franchise, said that was part of his goal with *CSI: Cyber*. "Our motto this season is: It can happen to you.... What I think is really, really great about *CSI: Cyber* in 2015 is that people will finally understand the consequences of how smart devices can be used for good and can be used for bad. You realize what's capable of happening and how to protect yourself as an undercurrent in the narrative. Ultimately, there's no better public service announcement."

Every minute of the day, people around the world create more than 204 million e-mails, 4 million Google searches, 100 hours of YouTube videos, and 300,000 tweets.

Keeping Up with the Digital World

Digital forensics experts are employed by many organizations, from law enforcement to private corporations. Large police departments might have their own computer crimes unit. Other digital forensics examiners work for state computer forensics labs or the FBI. Government agencies such as the National Security Agency (NSA), Department of Homeland Security (DHS), and U.S. military also employ

OPPOSITE: In 2002, the FBI created a special cyber division dedicated to investigating online crimes. Since then, the FBI has trained "cyber squads" of digital forensics experts and placed these agents in each U.S. field office.

digital forensics experts. Many private companies hire digital forensics experts as well. These experts identify criminal attacks against the company's networks. They also watch for employees using computers in ways that violate company policy. A number of digital examiners also work as private consultants to police departments, corporations, and individuals.

A college degree is not required for many jobs in digital forensics. Many digital forensics examiners start out with a career in law enforcement and then receive training in computer forensics. A minimum of a bachelor's degree is required to secure a position with the FBI or other federal agencies. Some positions require a graduate degree as well. Because technology is constantly changing, those in the digital forensics field must be willing to participate in continuing education. "This industry is

You Be the Analyst

When a file is encrypted, its data is changed into a coded message, or cipher. The change is made by following an algorithm. An algorithm is simply a set of instructions. A simple algorithm to encrypt a text file might be to shift each letter one space. In other words, we would replace each letter with the next letter in the alphabet. So the message "Digital forensics is fun," would become "Ejhjubm gpsfotjdt jt gvo." Write your own encryption algorithm. You can shift letters, add numbers, or come up with any set of instructions you want. When you are done, write a coded message. See if your friends or family can read it. Then give them the algorithm you used to encrypt the file. Can they decrypt your message?

ever-evolving. It's not the same day-in and day-out. You will need to engage with new technology," said Jonathan Rajewski, a computer forensics professor.

In addition to computer skills, digital forensics specialists need good communication skills. Once they've completed their analysis, they must write a report of their findings. It should be geared toward people who may be unfamiliar with technical computer terms. In addition, digital forensics experts are often called on to testify in court regarding their work on a case.

Cybercrimes are not always easy to prosecute, however. A large part of the problem is that up to 70 percent of all cybercrimes cross national borders. Many countries have different legal standards regarding what is considered a cybercrime. Because of this, some cybercriminals are never brought to justice. In 2000, for example, the "Love Bug" virus rapidly spread throughout North America, Europe, and Asia. It destroyed files, shut down e-mail servers, and scanned computers for usernames and passwords. All told, it caused billions of dollars in damage. The virus was tracked to hacker Onel de Guzman in the Philippines. But that country did not have any laws against computer hacking at the time. So de Guzman went unpunished.

More recently, cooperation among law enforcement agencies in the U.S. and abroad has led to the takedown of major international cybercrime operations. In April 2015, the FBI joined forces with the European Cybercrime Centre and the Dutch National High Tech Crime Unit. Together, these groups stopped the Beebone botnet, a malware program for stealing bank logins and passwords. Joseph Demarest Jr., assistant director of the FBI's cyber division, praised the international cooperation. "Botnets like Beebone have victimized users worldwide, which is why a global law enforcement team approach working with the private sector is so important," he said.

As they look for new ways to work together, digital forensics examiners are also preparing for the digital future. Some experts have expressed concerns about the use of cloud storage, which allows data to be stored online rather than on a device's hard drive. Experts fear that this will make it easier to hide or delete digital

evidence without leaving a trace.

Another innovation that worries some investigators is the solid-state drive (SSD). These drives store data in tiny transistors. When a file is deleted, the transistor on which it was stored is automatically erased. This means that investigators cannot recover deleted files from SSDs.

Digital forensics experts are also always on the lookout for new security threats. In 2015, they noted an increase in the use of ransomware. This is a form of malware that encrypts all the files on a computer. The user must pay a "ransom" fee in order to get the decryption key.

The very connectedness of the world of digital devices has some analysts concerned. Many corporations now allow (or even require) their employees to bring their own electronic devices to work. But opening the corporate network to outside devices only increases the system's exposure to attacks. This is part of a larger phenomenon known as the Internet of Things. The Internet of Things refers to all the "things" that are now connected to the Internet. Today, everything from fitness monitors to heating and cooling systems, vehicles, and even appliances are connected. But many of these devices offer little in the way of security protection.

nother future threat many in the digital forensics world are on the lookout for is cyberter-

rorism. Terrorists have long used the Internet to recruit followers, provide training, and plan attacks. But some worry that computers themselves may now become the weapons—and the targets—of a terrorist attack. By most definitions, cyberterrorism is a politically motivated attack against a computer system with the intention of causing harm or damage or influencing government policy. Cyberterrorists might use malware to disable critical **infrastructure**, such as a power grid or air traffic control system. "Terrorists can sit at one computer connected to one network and can create worldwide havoc," said Tom Ridge, former director of DHS. "[They] don't necessarily need a bomb or explosives to cripple a sector of the economy or shut down a power grid."

To date, there has not been an act of cyberterrorism in the U.S. And according to Maura Conway, a terrorism

and Internet researcher, there isn't likely to be one anytime soon. Other experts aren't so sure. They point out that many of the nation's critical infrastructure systems have inadequate security. And most are connected to the Internet.

Whatever the future may bring, one thing seems certain: technology will continue to play a vital role in our lives—and in crime. As quickly as technology develops, criminals find ways to exploit it. The future of crime solving may rest largely on the ability of digital forensics to keep pace with the changing face of the digital world. Doing so might just mean the difference between an unsolved mystery and bringing a criminal to justice.

Glossary

algorithms   procedures or sets of instructions to solve a problem

bit   short for binary digit, the smallest unit of digital data; all bits are either a 1 or a 0

botnet   a network of malware-infected computers that are controlled without the computer owners' knowledge

circumstantial   based on circumstances; not directly related to the fact in dispute but to related circumstances that might allow a conclusion to be inferred

DNA   abbreviation for deoxyribonucleic acid, a substance found in the cells that contains genetic information that determines a person's characteristics, such as eye color; when used in other contexts, DNA refers to something that identifies an object as unique

embezzle   to steal money, usually from an employer

extort   to use violence or threats to get something, such as money

infrastructure   the basic services and facilities needed to keep society functioning, such as power lines, schools, and roads

pixels   tiny dots that make up digital images

random-access memory (RAM)	computer memory that temporarily stores information used to carry out instructions and process data
registry	a computer database that stores information about applications, hardware, and users
routers	devices that transfer messages between computers
servers	main computers on networks, which store files, programs, and other data that is shared by other computers on the network
transistors	electronic devices that control the flow of electricity
viruses	forms of malware that attach themselves to files or programs that are then sent to other computers
worms	forms of malware that can make multiple copies of themselves and then send the copies to other computers; worms can replicate until they fill all the storage space on a device or network

Selected Bibliography

Cowen, David. *Computer Forensics: InfoSec Pro Guide.* New York: McGraw-Hill, 2013.

Doherty, Eamon P. *Digital Forensics for Handheld Devices.* Boca Raton, Fla.: CRC Press, 2013.

Easttom, Chuck, and Jeff Taylor. *Computer Crime, Investigation, and the Law.* Boston: Course Technology, 2011.

Maras, Marie-Helen. *Computer Forensics: Cybercriminals, Laws, and Evidence.* Burlington, Mass.: Jones & Bartlett Learning, 2015.

National Forensic Science Technology Center. *A Simplified Guide to Forensic Science.* http://www.forensicsciencesimplified.org/index.htm.

Ramsland, Katherine. *The C.S.I. Effect.* New York: Berkley Boulevard, 2006.

Sammons, John. *The Basics of Digital Forensics: The Primer for Getting Started in Digital Forensics.* 2nd ed. Waltham, Mass.: Elsevier, 2014.

Swanson, Charles R., Neil C. Chamelin, Leonard Territo, and Robert W. Taylor. *Criminal Investigation.* 9th ed. New York: McGraw-Hill, 2006.

Websites

FBI: Safe Online Surfing
https://sos.fbi.gov/

Play a game to see how much you know about staying safe on the Internet.

NSA Digital Media Center: CryptoKids
https://www.nsa.gov/kids/home.shtml

Learn more about codes and cybersafety.

Note: Every effort has been made to ensure that any websites listed above were active at the time of publication. However, because of the nature of the Internet, it is impossible to guarantee that these sites will remain active indefinitely or that their contents will not be altered.

Index

Aiken, Mary 52–53

algorithms 26, 67

BTK killer (Dennis Rader) 34

cybercrime victims 15, 16, 18, 19, 38, 40, 43, 56, 69

  Bloomberg 43

  Fidelity National Information Services 38, 40

  New York Times 16

  Sony Pictures 56

  Target 18

cybercrimes 11, 15–16, 18–19, 38, 40, 41, 42, 43, 53, 54, 56, 68–70, 74, 76

  and the Beebone botnet 69–70

  and the Love Bug 69

  and the Melissa virus 19

cybercriminals 15–16, 18, 31, 38, 40, 41, 42, 43, 44, 66, 68–69, 73–74, 76

  and cyberterrorists 73–74, 76

  de Guzman, Onel 69

  Ferris, Icarus Dakota 15

  Hacking for Girlies 16

  Mitnick, Kevin 16

  Zezev, Oleg 43

Department of Homeland Security (DHS) 65, 74

  Ridge, Tom 74

digital devices 10, 11–12, 14–15, 19–20, 23, 24, 35, 40, 42, 43, 44, 45, 47, 53, 70, 72–73

  and the Internet of Things 73

digital footprints 12, 14, 15, 35, 37, 42, 43–44, 45, 47, 56

  Internet Protocol (IP) addresses 42, 43–44, 56

digital forensics experts 10, 12, 19, 20, 24–26, 28, 31, 37, 40, 42, 44–45, 48, 57, 65–66, 68, 70, 72, 76

  Churchill, Matt 45

  Vance, Christopher 45

  Victor, Ira 12

Epstein, Kevin 53

evidence 10, 12, 14, 19, 20, 21, 23, 24–26, 28, 31, 34–35, 37, 40, 43, 45, 47, 48, 72

  and forensic images 25–26, 28, 45

Federal Bureau of Investigation (FBI) 33, 65, 66, 69–70

  Demarest, Joseph Jr. 69–70

  and the Dutch National High Tech Crime Unit 69

  and the European Cybercrime Centre 69

Forensic Outreach team 57–58

forensic tools 25–26, 29, 31, 34, 48, 54, 57

  and write blockers 25–26

law enforcement officials 11–12, 14, 19, 20, 21, 23, 34, 35, 44, 45, 47, 48, 65, 66, 69–70

legal proceedings 10, 14, 15, 59, 68–70, 76

McGuire, Melanie 35

National Academy of Sciences (NAS) 11

National Security Agency (NSA) 65

Pena, Kaue 57

Rajewski, Jonathan 66, 68

Sammons, John 12, 14

Shefrin, Ivan 54

Spikes, Branden 62

television and movies 50–54, 57–58, 59, 62

U.S. military 65

volatile artifacts 37–38

  and random-access memory (RAM) 38